RECITAL IN A PRIVATE HOME

Books by Eve Shelnutt

Poetry

Air and Salt
Recital in a Private Home

Fiction

The Love Child
Descant
The Formal Voice
The Musician

Critical

The Magic Pencil
The Writing Experience

Recital in a Private Home

poems by

Eve Shelnutt

Carnegie Mellon University Press
Pittsburgh 1988

ACKNOWLEDGMENTS

A number of these poems have appeared in the following magazines:
Art/Life; America; The Bellingham Review; Calapooya Collage; Cincinnati Poetry Review; Confrontation; Cape Rock; Cream City Review; North American Review; Ohio Journal; Passages North; South Dakota Review; South Florida Review; Z Miscellaneous.

The publication of this book is supported by grants from the National Endowment for the Arts in Washington, D. C., a Federal agency, and from the Pennsylvania Council for the Arts.

Library of Congress Catalog Card Number 88-70390
ISBN 0-88748-074-8

Printed and bound in the United States of America
First Edition

CONTENTS

With admiration and gratitude

To Shirley Clay Scott

To Ann Lyne

I

THE WORLD IMAGINES ITSELF BURNING

What better chancellery
than the house she holds
stretched in the hoop of her lap?
The minutest threads become a map
of all the cities she would go to,
not the largest, for the world
wants to begin its conflagration
small: a lamp overturning on a table
in Utah, kerosene spilling
into her husband's slippers,
one hand at her mouth
as she imagines oil-slick ponds,
black ducklings whose limp necks
rest like little boats on the shore,
their webbed feet bobbing.

So this is how it begins:
a house becomes a map
on which a pond sleeps under oil,
yellow feet making waves
as boats of feathers float.
A man cleans his slippers with a rag
but it is her house loosened from the hoop,
rainbow threads neatly cut and tied.
She comes in later, crying out,
wanting to kick at his slippers
for such an error, the limp rag
wadded in the fireplace
as the chill of her fury
seeps into her useless fingers.
He lights the house.

AT THE CONVENT SCHOOL LIBRARY

Did someone scream?
It seemed someone screamed,
a thrumming sound
like the end of a Beethoven storm,
a keening, a red pulsing flower.
But let the flower burn. Murmur:
Why is it like it is
and, Why do we have to care.
So many useless facts!
Do you know how they use bamboo
in Malaya? Why the alligator's
blades open more often in sunlight?
Oh gorgeous girls, we help each other,
and here we are, starched in linen,
black bows at our sleek necks,
ears twitching to sleep.
Tomorrow we have reports, everywhere
words foaming or shuddering like waves:
sedimentary, metamorphic, our
teeth hunching, small stones
on the cold shore of our tongues.
It is a long baptism,
everything above us fluttering
plaintive calls: Float.
Empty things float.
But we are filling.
What else do we not hear,
sound becoming weight?
And if the flower must burn,
let it swing like a pole star
above the logic of water.

ONE SELECTED

As Mary's wet sponge
wipes awe from Joseph's forehead
and Christ turns to rest
the tiny body through which
all sins must pass,
Peter will know it has commenced:
the journey to no greater shame
than to have done his part,
alert to rustling of feathers,
variations so minutely learned
he hears each egg cry.
"Not you," he whispers,
candling sorrow's immaculate shape,
releasing the hens to innocence
until, at Easter, he believes
he loves everything that flies.

THE BLIND MEN OF ST XAVIER

How light the wings
of innocence
blocking so little sun.
We see by heat,
even you
and at first
you will not be conscious
of the growing
weight of wings.
You'll tell me,
you'll tell me all the same,
in winter
when the sun is weakest.
One pale afternoon
you will wait for Cecile,
feathers dewy with love
or fear of love
torn away like a nest.
Pacing, eating seeds
from your pockets,
listening to the clock
striking the hour
the nuns reopen the gate...
such wingspan!
And the next afternoon,
pacing, chewing,
your shadow
will be heavier.
One day you will shade
your eyes with feathers,
believing you see her
whirring toward you.
This is how you will join
the blind of St Xavier.
You'll maybe say,
Many women use the same scent.
Shall I answer what I think?
It is the same sort of sadness.
It will tell us,
It will tell us all the same.

AT LITTLE SISTERS OF THE POOR

I.
Our patient worries us
as his heart knocks on his chest,
the fever asleep like a crocus
under a field of skin so soft
it should be an easy flowering.
Where is its will, its
subterfuge? We are
busy women, our caps need
starching, someone must go
buy more glass straws and
outside the gate a dog
whines pitifully. Let this child's
forehead break open,
not for us but for all
the little ones who suffer,
not the least of which
is this flower wanting out.

II.
All night we dabbed at his forehead
as if it were a wine stain
and now we have tamped him down
where wily roots lift the
headstones after a month of rain.
No, we won't return to see
his one name listing
like a ship on high water.
We talk and talk:
what was wrong with
our little vanities?
We could have taught him
to braid baskets, sandals.
Must virtue proceed from absence?
Some nights our hands burn
like souls which have left our bodies,
a relentless solicitation,
an anarchy of love.

CIVIL ENGINEER IN SPAIN

In my cave I found a sluice
which I hid behind a blanket
hung by pegs in the wet clay,
I'm not sure why. It was mine
in a foreign country, a flag, say,
or currency in a local bank.
It was merely a trickle
but when I brought Maria home with me
to make love, it seemed to grow
as if its source were bottomless.
Perhaps she heard it,
perhaps it was she who told them,
the men who have lived
all their lives in drought,
not travelers as I am
for whom water is a body
to be crossed by air.
I did not love her, that is true,
although I said the words.
And they came, mid-morning,
four of them, huge and jealous,
and they tossed me in the empty well
where my tongue swelled by noon
to twice its size and, by the next,
a bulb outside my lips. And, seeing
this flower, they pulled me out.
I agreed, gesturing, to build a cistern
since now I knew how a wordless body fills.
And Maria has returned, beautiful as ever.
After all, I am the man who built the cistern.
I say nothing and, on its own, it deepens.

PROGRESS OF THE ESTATE ROAD

Ladies' silk brushing
hand-laid bricks
on the half-circle
cupping the house.
A man with his level
stooping in moonlight.
Acorns dropping
like the rattle of a sistrum.
The shadow of a skein
one late morning.
On the edges of four bricks,
lichen, a beginning.
Then, coarse rain,
part ice, and the brick
contracts, a winter riff.
So many bald heads
leaning to the fire.

SHAKING THE SMALL, SYMBOLIC HEAVEN

In Bath County, ferrets are crocheting snow,
a competition of inching scarves,
ends flipping in the breeze of horses
practicing runs at Litgow Farm,
a ladies' club of hooves to shake
crystals in the tent where houses camp
facing forward, raffle tickets stacked
high in the midway booths, owls
on night guard circling deer who gather
preening at the rink, hooves sharp,
tulle tufts spinning while otters
clap the ice, wind howling drunk
against naked trees on which buckets hang
filling with our sweet sins.

AGAIN

Light feeds snow
bedding down receptive,
contagion of mindless sleep
after falling play,
each shapely invention
erotic articulation:
mound obscuring needles,
limbs, torn leaves
over which you will roll
a perambulator of rust,
broken spokes, tires flapping,
pushing Cassandra as if each flake
offered impeccability. Oh
the pity of self-prophecy
which will not take. You think
to place her there, in snow,
as if she too would become
finally rain itself. Summer
you will walk a beach
waiting for clouds to gather,
proud father of misfortune
cleansed. Priam, again
you miss the lesson of snow.

A CUNEIFORM IN ITALY

Why does the baker's wife
run back and forth
across the little square
from his oven with its
dancing flame
to the blacksmith's bellows,
his anvil a metronome
in cinnamon time?
What is the horse thinking,
hung in its pillory
as it bucks with
stiffening flanks?
What is the small boy doing
other than cooking
raw balls of dough on twigs
over a charcoal fire?
The sky above the bakery
is always the same but for
a subtle aging of light.
Sadness is burning here,
a new eclipse.
Would the blacksmith
speak to the baker's wife, ever?
Does the blacksmith notice
the sky above him darkens
with every nail?
And would the baker kill him,
her crumpled handkerchief
drifting from her open hand
across the little square?

BONNARD REVISING

So the laundry girl, unaware that her life
spent in the odor of bleach is being watched,
receives a dog who has grown spots
since his sketchy life began on her right,
walking as if to leave a scene so gray
nothing would come of remaining.
Now he is dressed
for something, loping past her on the left
with his head down as if he knows
what is coming is not
the toss of bones from the basket
hanging almost to her black shoes.
She is lucky it has not rained
for the umbrella she uses as a cane
has a twisted spike.
In the sketch you could see it moving across paper.
Now he has remembered the square stones
on which it broke; it may not rain.

The wind-whipped trees are missing;
a French door stands where gray leaf bent,
glass an irridescent black.
"If only you knew,"
says Bonnard, "what trouble I have drawing things!"
Which is what I would tell my sister
waiting as the sky stills for a bus
that will hit also the dog just outside
the frame where she stands politely formless.
Otherwise, of course,
he would open the French door,
draw inside someone like our mother
alive, pouring tea as the rain
decides where to fall.

I would tell the laundry girl who will be
first to cradle my sister's head:
There is still time to give up the work
of discovering stains,
but he did not like the canvas
wearied by the brush.

II

RECITAL IN A PRIVATE HOME

Rooms of green silks and velvet
changing color as if to music,
two maids bringing acrid tea
on silver trays, our feet
wrapped around chair legs in the
shape of snakes, leaving a stigmata
on each ankle; *Charlotte,*
the beautiful maid; but the Lady's
husband is dead and has been dead
for all of this distressing time
of music bought by women who inherit,
the men having so specified,
rising up against starched linen
to sign with long and lovely fingers
how beauty is to be fostered
when the body goes, so Charlotte, too,
plays a little. "Do we all not
play a little?" the Lady asks,
among too many porcelain pieces,
beside an escritoire far too tall,
and we are edgy, but it is Sunday,
Sunday afternoon, to be exact.
The monks, I say, the monks should have
fished him out when he died.

THE ART OF OWNING OBJECTS OF BEAUTY

Mrs. Chauncey McCormick of Chicago
who owns Van Gogh's "Fishing in Springtime"
pauses before the canvas as she leaves the house
for tea with the ladies, asking as she is driven
why the second boat is drifting empty
as the man in the first ties flies.
Lemon sharp in her mouth at the Grand Hotel
she counts humble fish on the green plate
of the boat, wondering, too, why he painted
poles hemming each skiff, two for the fisherman,
a pair for the empty boat upon which Van Gogh
fears setting foot in springtime in 1887
when the sun is normal in size, flowers
small and pale. The river, she remembers,
is almost flat, feathers of blue, and the bridge,
as in Japanese prints, arches gently.
But it is early and, if she shivers in her fur,
it is the air, not time ruffling the Seine
for she does not own that painting,
Mrs. Chauncey McCormick of Chicago.

SEURAT, 1887

To clothe the idea
in perceptible form
merely with the eye
not the midriff
of the mind, here
is the model seen
from behind, such
light as there is
pocking the skin
blue, flesh-tone
pressing it
against you as she
sits on the green bed
pebbled in yellow.
Her head tilts forward
from the long neck;
it is possible
to trace the spine
of light to her ears
tucked into black hair.
Before her are hatchings
of vermillion and pink,
walls without let-up
so she has no place
to go if she wanted
but remember
the bed is green
and yellow, and
to divide tones
is to take advantage
of all the benefits
deriving from color
and harmony:
the mixture of pure pigments,
the choice of
brushstroke
commensurate with
the size of the canvas.

TRANSFORMED BY WIND

Horses nuzzle empty bowls
near the girl whose fingers
outline a church,
back straight against
a knobby pew, scattered slices
of lemon at her feet,
flakes of desire drifting
past her open coat;
beneath the cloth
the sound of stirring.

So the girl eats cubes of sugar,
naming horses as they roll
their silvery flanks
against collection plates,
handsome deacons bagging
themselves by the creamery
while seasons thunder, shake,
part into walls of tea,
divide into madelines.
How lovely to be served.

JEWELS

This is the tower wherein
males of the species
perch on rafters waiting
for the stone floor
to ignite in color:
amethyst, gold,
purple on a black cloth,
shafts of morning light
angling at the leaded
window where bees
gauze the air with humming
as gray feathers
burst upon us tipping
until we spill
into the chamois of desire.

"LUXE, CALME AND VOLUPTE" by Matisse

Feeding the body is for men
whose memory is not composed
of pinpricks of color sliding
like sand to water.
But these four bathers
recline by an empty cloth
where points of light
coalesce around a woman
combing her hair in
deliberate innocence.
How could they not follow
tremors of her predilection
to the sea where the merest dune
of mountains separates the sky,
sea-colored and flowing?
The sun so rapturous,
the woman so empirical,
how could she not lift,
her legs, a v pointing west
into heat, the men rising
in formation, a skein of lovers
looking down for a cloth of fish
and a mermaid combing her hair?
The sky is doubly voluptuous,
concrete, alarming, shiver
after shiver.

ARTIST PAINTING ORCHID AND HORSE

Slumbrous odor
in the orchid's eye
petal defining
sweat-slick flanks
in green houses
pasture of third
lips enlarged
light bluish-red
cantering
into the trumpet
belly of hay
inching up hills
in colt-time
sweet fur
harnessing
women profusely wild.

NEED FOR ALLEGORY

Behind trellises of rose,
lattice-work of hedge,
a yawning pavement of heat,
our houses sit in shade,
curtains pulled tight,
air humming with insects,
bird wings blue and rust.

What did Breughel know
of the desolate street
where a dog's three-quarter lope
would make us edge the light?
"Two Monkeys", though austere,
does not count: huge chains,
one monkey's eyes arching
perfectly to mirror the arch
behind their heads,
for the artist gives himself
hope in such symmetry.

We need his gardeners
drunk on women in bangles
strung like a fence
along the road,
children in pairs
scudding crutches up the walk,
two goiters dangling
from every maid's neck,
twin rookeries of sin,
pain we can touch at the stump,
not this green fragility.

MICHELANGELO SKETCHING

You offer the body newly
on a table under lights
so bright each vein opening
announces its willingness
to pilot as we crawl
into our skiffs of hope
to know it even
in uncharted regions
where we are sure a house
sits under unusual trees
wherein a place is set,
food we have never tasted
hot or icy in bowls,
silver bearing new initials
verifying a marriage
you invite us to bless
as you raise a glass
to beauty
lifting her skirts for death.

BIBLIOGRAPHY, for John Woods

Though born in Indiana, he has lived in Michigan
since 1955 where, across the tundra all poets
grow in their minds, tractors have thundred
to ring his house, last outpost of memory:
such labor women's hands flutter like thread
on their bosoms from which boys swing to war,
fathers waving from rows of Depression glass
catching sun the widower slides beneath at the rectory
as the organist raises her chorus, billowing pipes
to loosen the brother, dead, who walks where apples
bruise the orchard, alcohol spouting from the root
of impatience, so many tractors awaiting the cavalry
of love.

FOR THE PIANIST RECENTLY DECEASED

Death's arrangement
in impossible time
meant composers for hands
and the spine swaying
went immediately on tour
or to tea with dowagers
whispering even to tourmalines:
Raise high the baton of hope
or pass the absinthe.
She was, ah,
pianissimo/fortissimo in one.
You think divas are rare
who chew garlic
as love inflames their throats,
ribs' air forging
dramas of iron? Who
but the pianist
stops the symphony's
clashing on the hill?
She lifts one hand
and they decamp to study the plan.
She ignites in humble silence,
burning at the stake
of our genius.
Then they lumber up
squinting
as she slips
through the needle's eye.

SHOPPING IN MARCH

Two men walk the aisles.
One of them is a doll,
the knob of his head
turning his face toward sleep,
a slow creaking.
The other is a string bag
which holds the doll,
the jars, the beaujolais.
The doll's fat
ripples his belly
but the string bag is taut.
He has done lifting
for pleasure in winter.
The doll's knees
as he tried to learn
probably ached for months,
he is so short.

Their dogs, who do not yet
synchronize, cause the men
to dance in the parking lot.
The doll's face turns awake,
expression startled,
as if he might fall or,
having fallen, forget to cry.
Soon spring will loosen
its scarf of snow,
blooms massaging the neck.
By August something new
will struggle out,
warm skin slick.
Its head will be knobless,
mouth forever open.

THE SNAKE HUNTER'S APPRENTICES

Let us learn the final art
of skinning.
Each morning our breath
uncoils from our ribs,
words like sacs of poison
quiver on our tongues.
It is dangerous to leave us
knowing half of anything.
At noon when the sun is closest,
our foreheads grow hoods,
brush weaves around as we rise
to strike, often, at nothing.
Yet how gently we would stretch
the silken skins on the ground.
At night we would lie by them
lending our heat. Our breath
would slither in high grass,
dreams would cease their hissing.
Even you, one arm deep
in such silence, would find
snake-bracelets heal
one who has learned everything.

NIGHT WAILS

Night wails pitifully
until she puts its head
to one nipple, whispering
All is water, then
sets it drifitng
where the day's swift current
takes it safely to women
kneeling among water-weeds
where they bend to unwrap
the light blankets,
place it naked on the ground.
It rises slowly to follow
children down dirt lanes,
their hoops like fishes'
mouths opening for bait.
Its face is smudged with dust,
the juice of apples. Seeds
of pomegranates speckle
its cheek. By noon no one
would know its lineage,
and, lying in the high bed
of her lover, she whispers
All is water as he kisses
sweetness from her lips.
Then light fades, pulling her
by both hands. She looks down
remembering sand in striped
shadows, seaweed trailing
from the crab's closed fists,
her own hands crawling.
Its eyes close once
as it rests by a tree.
It almost cries out but the wind
lifts as she sails to snatch it
from the willow's grip. She hums
as last heat warms the soft spot
pulsing in its head, and it watches
the pining world with shuttered eyes.
Oh, for love, she cries, I almost
lost it, and to the sound
it knows best, it nuzzles her chest,
sucking dreams of water from her breasts.

III

DEATHS OF MOTHERS

Three blue-haired ladies descend a hill,
draw tight against high wind
brown velvet curtains and light a fire.
We settle in to their needles squeaking
on the tapestry, their creaking shoes,
rub of cotton hose, learning by sound
how death winters: weather worse
than ice scaling windows, twigs
tapping brittle feet against the door.
We comb fire through our hair, believe
even a brush can burn with hope,
until the ladies finally sigh, pick yarn
of every color from their shoes, pair them
by the bank, sink into the pond of spring,
after which we are left to braid
our tufted hair and twitter.

DEATHS OF MOTHERS II

Sisters, he is waiting,
that last potentate
who picks his teeth,
sweeping clean a circle
where she is to sit
for inspection,
so heavy a tapestry
around her he will
salivate, teeth itch
as he fingers our
silk curves
as we raise sail
for the hidden cove,
her life, spread on the deck,
so bright he is momentarily
blinded, his rage
when he recovers
that which drowns us now.

DEATHS OF MOTHERS III

With one hand she is timing
her forehead, such contractions
of the brain it opens. Soon
she will reach in like a mid-wife
to draw us out bellowing,
our sucking mouths wordless,
fists balls of light on her chest,
tiny feet dangling shoeless
on her belly so empty
she will feel hunger again.

DEATHS OF MOTHERS IV
for Shirley

I.
You cannot remember the house
in which a mother drew you from her
though you have sketched porches
to cover any facade.
Now you take a novel view,
a transmutation, a domain
where love would be identical
with the silence of lizards.

II.
If only sweat were black,
a scalding cape filling
as you dive: nothing, nothing
on the bottom but scenes
ossified in silt,
a bone metamorphosis
undulating slowly, a deserted
battlefield trembling in water.

III.
Then a mother's body arches,
its will sweeping with broad strokes,
the soul rising on a vacuum
through which such light pours
you imagine you are mended,
a fantastic reward, your head
growing more and more painful
having surfaced so quickly for air.

IV.
How many eyes close forever
next to us, while we, longing
for the crowning achievement,
find sleep shot through
with tomorrow's love?
There was no body, only
a drop of blood added
to the world's nocturnal sea.

THE LONG MOURNING

For three months
I belonged to neighbors
through whose embroidered curtains
sun filtered rosettes of pain
moving in the breeze.
I pictured my mother
exposed to the water's glare
like a dolphin leaping.
My heart followed her; I lay
with my head at the foot of the bed
as if leeward in a boat.
My lips tasted salt.
Father sat in the bow,
hands cupping his face.
His beard was wet and hard.
On shore we left wet footprints
between a row of wailing women.
Dun-colored beasts rose from the sand.
They were not my mother
lifted far from grassy banks,
the water weeds of penitence.
Her form, like fog, rippled
again to sea. She waved or beckoned.
I saw her hands were scrubbed to the bone
with bitterness and awe. One day
a neighbor slapped me;
a terrible creature fell into her lap,
clawing at her skirt. They gave me wine
in tiny spoons. I felt dizzy with power.
It was the imitation of love
which carried me back,
a faint sigh or creaking
as if the boat rowed itself in sleep.
The door was not completely shut:
my mother cast a shadow, pink,
keeping a vigil in my dark room.
Blissfully I lay beside her, wrapped
in her subtle emanations
as wind beat against
the white shutters of death.

THE POETS LABOR AT OUR MOTHER'S DEATH

They gather
to the slough of her breath
as her neck arches swanlike,
arms spread featherlight,
this body a novation
they have studied
in a dream of words.
Each has brought a chair
or stool or hammock,
bed of string or nails,
arranged at angles
on the weathered porch
beyond which lie
heavens of persiflage
and she is not deaf.
So they dream her life
as she would have it,
full of light and music.
They wake refreshed
and, lifting her body,
bear it to the hill.

WOMAN WAITING

Rouge thick for the welcoming
imprint of lips, hers flat
under delicate pink, composed
as though she awaits a train,
eyes shut against sulfurous fume,
hands crossed over what would be
her purse. How prim! Her stillness
does not say she fears the tunnel
beyond the long stairs for which
she wears new shoes, black, sturdy.
And if she does not send cards
saying, Wish you were here,
or photographs of her leaning
almost invisible into his black coat,
who is to question her discretion,
Death needing so many wives.

SENTENCE

Daily he enters the alley on stilts
since, having died, he will not wear shoes
nor fill my cup against enormous thirst,
sun burning the stripe of his stilts on my face
turned upward for the question which always comes:
What did you expect, a horse, a rope, my arms
grown muscled for pulling down the bars? Oh
death has made him bitter, such freedom a brother
might have had were I not alive and wooing
jailers with a smile I shed
when night snuffs heat from my cell
where I coil warming on half a heart,
breathing lightly and waiting.

AT THE MASS GRAVEYARD

The dead have no doubt
that something overwhelming
has happened. They disclose
a sort of detachment,
consuming oblivion.
If they talk,
surely it is of weight:
leaves, moss, myrtle,
white violets, stones.
To carve a branch
breaking over stone
is to lighten them,
yet, for us, the branch
is endlessly breaking.
There is no wretchedness
like flogged men,
but why speak of wounds?
The dead wear no stigmata.
In this whole plain
there is no blood,
only our memories
of their discarded arms,
the train's rumbling,
each like the tooth
of a rake. Here and there
a child is held up
to the narrow opening,
a little blue enamel mug
dancing with every jolt.

OBITUARY, Robert Stallman, 1980 (after words by Jean Leymarie and George Riviere)

Space forbids me giving
a detailed account
of his final evolution
but generally speaking
after 1970
the interlude of doubt
soul-searching over
he reverted with
few exceptions
to the ideals
of his youth
but amplified now
cosmic, visionary
handled with
utter freedom
consummate technical
mastery. His
still life has
something solemn
in its utter truthfulness
because he himself
is deeply moved
by nature.

LANDSCAPE AND FIGURE

Summer, the sun leaned back
in its rind of fire. Months
I did not see you. Tonight
snow offers up shadow of deer
sensing; one accurate rush
of anything metallic
flattens the body, heart beating
on the ground to let it in.

You knew the word *scalpel,* mouth,
when it was named, a black O
to let them in, you were
more innocent than deer.
How do we know in death the body
transforms itself? I saw you
beckoned. I saw you touch
their ears, quivering.

And that was you in the clearing,
head poised above the salt lick.
Let them teach you now.

INVITATION TO THE ORCHARD
for Harry, 1939-1980

Then, sleep strained at the bit,
blue mane shaking stars
across the gabled roof, odor of fox
filling the stall as I trembled
until you streaked the orchard.

Always they healed, welts
where branches scraped my face,
desire the crop's wet tongue
licking my flanks at the stile,
such leaping apples fell.

Yes, Death calls the hound
whose howling wakes more dead.
They scramble up some nights
filling every tree. And you, so
newly treed, have the brightest eyes.

Observe, then, how I lead, sorrow
blanketing our backs were trophies ride.
We will ring the tree with gold,
and what hunter could object:
sleep betrothed to foxes?

ORCHARD WINTER

To select death
is to uncrate the apples
of our mouths,
let them roll across
a blanket of frost,
the original,
eaten to the core,
lodged like a filling
in one tooth,
it was that hard.

To select death
is to shake children
from the crooks of our arms,
and let the wind
prune us to almost
nothing: a twig
for walking down
the narrow rows.
Surely, as Eve imagined,
the orchard ends!

If love is hard and crisp,
let rotting apples
soften the earth
from which we pull our roots.
The hole is not for burial.
Fill it with seeds,
then hang a smudge pot
from my waving hand.
I want to go in smoke
seeking the killing frost.

THE DEMONIC BOY OF RAPHAEL'S TRANSFIGURATION

I am the boy of time
the Disciples gather around

disregarding all proportions,
a handful of sugar in their pockets.

This is your family.
Loves us.

So I must lean backwards,
never letting go.

Sometimes I follow a circling hawk,
sometimes the brief moments

of carnal love, its wings
like a stiff fan unfolding.

So you see how creation
can turn against us,

a savoured flame,
a deceptive splinter of dawn?

Madness shoulders the universe.
Secrets drift like sugar from its hands.

IV

ANSWERING

If you write for company,
why limit yourself to women of seventy?
In my bedroom is a faded rug,
rose-patterned; pictures of my
greatgrandmother line the bureau
and I grow more like her daily.
A rocker can be set rocking.
We could undress by candlelight
or kerosene, wick trimmed close,
the odor of sulphur binding the quilts.
As for me, I do not like taut skin.
A man once showed me
how the leopard's rides loosely
over his muscles, and why,
although I need not tell you
of countries other than our own:
how she is exhausted
climbing from the wagon,
so much of herself left littering
the dry plains when axles broke,
and how, when he offers his hand,
she does not think of age,
her children left beside stones.
Nor will she name them
as if tapping her heart three times
to get it going. It beats: a code
which only the novice cannot read,
as if smoke were merely smoke
instead of news. And he does this:
he builds a fire of twigs
and helps her bathe, riding the cloth
gently. Wraps her in coarse blankets
bartered by those whose time also
is ending. He may hum a song
for she likes words still and watchful.
Listen! And do you see how she smiles,
a small animal half-asleep in his lap,
absently nuzzling her open hand?

BOTH WAYS

As we walked, pebbles
stinging our calves, I announced:
We are trespassing; even grasshoppers
fly up in warning. Adding:
You see how hostile the world is,
pushing us with water into the mountains
which open to anoint us with ash?
Once I stayed out all night,
once in all these years,
and I have never spoken of what happened
but all the same, I am furious,
a mute avowal in me.
Life is not a little black chair
with roses painted on it. Perhaps
we handle great symbols too lightly.
But you pointed to a tree across the road,
shading a circle the wind had made,
the smooth ground singing.
I am a woman of two faces.
When I am obviously leaning,
for death has, finally, the stronger pull,
watch me turn one face your way again.

I KNEW A MAN

I knew a man who was not beautiful;
that was the point of my fever:
to break out in spots until he claimed
his disease, a diagnosis of sorts,
he had been lingering so long.
My body was the amnesiac's map
which he unrolled, city of filthy
children on dirt lanes, a Calcutta
of maimed limbs bearing the imprint
of their mother's knives, they were
so desperate when he left them.
He cried on my thighs, washed himself
in the Ganges of my flowing tongue;
I was Victoria and Lady Mountbatten
in one. But, ah, a country claims you.
And we have stayed on.

ANNA, RAVENING

On the third try
I married a good man.
It took me years to suspect
he was as good as dead;
an image, like a tablet
inscribed with laws
or a tombstone, the body simply
flat, also a graceful pose except
it lacks sustaining interest.

If I opened my mouth wide enough
speaking in tongue of love
in any form,
five warts wobbled there,
sin panting like dogs in the undergrowth.

Where, then, since I have earned it,
is my red taffeta slip
huge and thin as gauze?
Why does the sky not open
in a wash of pink?

LITTLE BEACH, for Joe

It was for pecans I loved you
that 12th year of my submerged life,
and for your mother's oven,
square of light enclosed,
its slats of heat. How slick
their tanned little bodies,
faces creased in concentration,
arms and legs invisibly tucked,
backs curved for the long dive
spiraling. To send down so many
divers leaping from the precipice
of your hand! How could I not love you,
so many broken for the sake of my hunger?

ALTHEA, WHO NEVER SANG
LOUIE, ALMOST ALL HEART

Althea always talked,
applied ointment to her lips,
kept on talking
without knowing why
but otherwise was lovely
and, blessed
with all that vanity
like a cavern
or a warm bath
or finding six fish
side by side
in the middle of a road
when haze covers the sky,
she never really looked
at Louie with his pea-sized
lungs strung close to a heart
the size of twin persimmons
stuffed in a cage, who
asked himself why
Althea was singing
and would he fall
if the singing stopped.

SECOND BEGINNING, IN AIR

As fish
I was loved for scales
reflecting desire.
But who reads beauty
in the half-transformed,
the scythe, for instance,
before the coming of grass
or the apple pulsing
on Adam's mute rib?
Beneath the first tree
is a book of names
working to the surface
where love hides in shade.
I will choose one
from the culture of water
and, if you call it,
I will scatter light
from the fixed and distant
point of my becoming.

SOURCE: THE MIRAGE

Years, it has been retreating:
the dazzling sheets of cotton
spread at the foot of mountains;
pediments of October fire;
rows of peach trees marching
like slaves into sun-beaten shacks;
purple muscadines wrapping pines
into bundles by stagnant water;
our house set beneath willows
scouring the ground;
swing tipping its plank of light
on nights of heat-lightning;
behind the house, broken wire
pinging against metal posts,
birds perching from habit mid-air
on the taut line of absence.

DAUGHTERS WEIGHING THEIR LEGACY

He named us
with such care
we carry our names
as others have worn
the blue tattoo.
Men lift our wrists as if to kiss them;
instead, read hunger, thirst.
History touches even
horses' teeth,
the selling point,
where stained hay dangles
to suggest an enclosed yard,
the cart, its load of women
who once had names.
If passion is to win,
we must be fed madness:
bones gathering bones
for a fire of lutes,
lily-smoke rising,
two kinds of thirst,
our wrists opening white
in moonlight, spilling
over stone hieroglyphics,
over bent grass, swelling
like a bow wave over crumbling
red earth. And the sun
when it rises, relentless.

HAVING IMAGINED

A boy and girl hold to the door
as if to anchor it, her tendrils
in an almost imperceptible breeze
grazing the gnats who wait to enter
the caves of their mouths where words
anticipate the invention of shame.

The boy has his father's eyes, which,
although his head is perfectly still,
circle the landscape. Behind them
the mother irons in scorched air
and from red hills buzzards
cite nothing actually dead.

Weeds tumble across the last dog's
tracks, sun shellacs rocks, leaves
of sunflower, the empty flatbed truck.
What could the father's letter
do to them? Even the boy could cry,
enameling his cheeks, body crusting.

The girl's hair would spark, setting
her face aflame, words marking the door.
Imagining a scow moving through dust,
the father lifts his letter from the box
and, as if dust were water parting,
walks through holy to the other side.

FATHER STILL ON HORSEBACK

He carries only words
softening the floors of stalls;
on himself only the patrician nose
lit to authenticate a dukedom
of castles on the hill.
In daylight he scatters petals
on the forest floor,such
sweetness women fall. Yes,
he loves his country dearly.
He campaigns for light in each window,
every chimney freeing the smoke of roses.

IS THIS THE SEA?

To subdue the long-gone event
I call it *horse* as if to ride elevated
through waves searing minutest nicks of shell,
welts of seagrass, kiss of knotted burrs.
Oh the counter-rhythm of your body cresting
beneath its cloven hooves! Yes, you liked
love's endless tumult. But the breathless
horse asks, "Is this why the new moon
holds the old under his arm?"
It seems I must place you, as on a post card,
moored off Cape May in dusk's loosening braid,
night, if you should remember me,
filling the space where my name would be.
We, the horse and I, the horse
who does not need a place fixed like a star,
walk side-by-side, our breaths played out
by the hook of light. We take up oars
and look! It is a wondorous sight: the sea,
the little boat, two beasts rowing.

THERE IS A STREAK OF QUIET MELANCHOLY

There is a streak of quiet melancholy
in my sisters' spirits. The slightest
allusion to music brings tears to their
eyes though their intelligent faces
never change. Sometimes they agree
by signal when to cry, and instruments
take up their places at the music stands.
Gondolas floated in the moonlit harbour
when our parents met; a slow recovery
was taking place. "Why do you stare so?"
our mother asked, and Father, with a
thousand caresses, rowed to shore.
We must realize that not a soul knows
who he really is. Calmly we must sit
at the organ bench when a storm breaks
and play the work we see open there.
Let us put down our napkins and stare
across the room. Who is rowing?
Yet when the music begins, slowly
they put their hands over their bowed heads.

IT IS SNOWING

It is snowing
on the memory

of our father
rising unscaleable

although my sisters
offer to climb

into claws of rock.
Such passion!

I have thought to write
a critical guide

of their sorrow
for I watched them

select rope, picks,
layers of clothing.

But just as I knelt
beside the coffin

I saw opposite me
their pale young faces

the play of light
struggling to be free.

The mirror was covered
in a black cloth.

In the whole room
only their eyes shone.

They were like dolls
breaking themselves apart

to discover what was inside.
No, they won't climb

to a still lake
hidden in the peaks.

Snow erases all shadow;
an angel rises

without blemish.
Even in the night

it shines as brightly
as our consciousness.

Fathers, I tell you,
are like that

in their ruthless demands.
You cannot go blind.

This spotless blood
will redeem you

come Spring: water
as you wash your

dolorous little faces
will whisper:

I have a fear of solitude.
Memory will drip from your hands.